2
hatsu haru
Shizuki Fujisawa

CONTENTS

hatsu haru 2

KAI ICHINOSE

A lover of women and the most popular boy in school. A high school first-year. He and Takanashi fight like cats and dogs, but...!?

RIKO TAKANASHI

A tomboy. A classmate of Kai's since elementary school who has absolutely no interest in him. Currently has a crush on Suwa-sensei.

SUWA-SENSEI

The assistant teacher of Kai and Riko's class. Like an older brother to Riko.

STORY

● Kai is the school's most popular playboy, who can almost always be found fooling around with girls like there's no tomorrow. One day, he learns that Riko Takanashi, a violent and conceited girl he's known since childhood, has a crush on Suwa-sensei.

● An unexpected look at her softer side causes a strange emotion to swell within Kai...Is this love!? Kai tries to figure it out, but when he sees how close Riko is with Suwa-sensei, he starts to suspect that they are already dating.

● Riko falls ill at school and Kai ends up carrying her home. There he learns that her love is unrequited, and he can't contain his excitement. At this moment, Kai finally realizes that he is in love with Riko.

● On the class camping trip, Kai finds himself alone under the stars with Riko. In an attempt to kiss her, he orders her to close her eyes, and then...!?

Thank you very much for picking up HATSU * HARU, Volume 2!
z z z
Lately, I've been in trouble because I love my futon too much.
Futon

CHAPTER 5

hatsu haru

—HEY.
DOKI (BADMP)
ドキッ
WHY ARE YOU CRYING?
...I FORGOT MY CALLIGRAPHY SET......
...AND I ALWAYS FORGET IT.
SENSEI'S GONNA YELL AT ME AGAIN...
......

—HERE.
WHAT...? YOU'RE LETTING ME BORROW IT!?
UH-HUH.
IT'S NOT LIKE I NEED IT RIGHT NOW.
THANK YOU!
ARE YOU STUPID?

WE HAVE WRITING CLASS NOW TOO.
WHAT ARE YOU GONNA DO?
SHUT UP.
LEAVE ME ALONE.
I'LL BE FINE.
I DON'T CARE IF I GET YELLED AT.

THAT DAY...
...TAKANASHI QUIETLY FINISHED THE EXTRA WORK SHE GOT ASSIGNED AS PUNISHMENT FOR FORGETTING HER CALLIGRAPHY SET.
TAKANASHI HAS ALWAYS, ALWAYS BEEN LIKE THIS.

SHE ALWAYS PUTS OTHER PEOPLE FIRST.
—IF THESE FEELINGS WOULD DESTROY SOMETHING PRECIOUS TO ME, I'D RATHER KEEP THEM LOCKED UP FOREVER.
THAT'S WHY, OUT OF CONCERN FOR SUWA...
...SHE'S LETTING HER HOPELESS CRUSH GROW.
BUT ...

...THAT DOESN'T WORK FOR ME.

....
I TOLD YOU TO CLOSE YOUR EYES.
...WHY SHOULD I?
BIKU (WINCE)

DAMN, YOU'RE SLOW.

MISHI (CRUNCH)
!?
YOOO-OUUU AAARE ...
GIRI (GRIND)
GIRI
GIRI
GIRI
...SOOOO...
JUST BECAUSE WE'RE SITTING HERE...
...IN A ROMANTIC LOCATION, UNDER A SKY FULL OF STARS...

YOU'LL TAKE ANY WOMAN WHO'S BREATHING, YOU HORNY TOAD!!!?
KUA (ROAR)
N... NO...!
I—
I WANTED YOU!
UM!
...UH, UM...
GASA (RUSTLE)
THERE!! YOU'VE GOT A CALLER!
PROBABLY SOME GIRL CONFESSING HOW MUCH SHE LOVES YOU AGAIN!
GUI (YANK)
IF YOU WANNA DO STUFF LIKE THIS, GO FIND SOMEONE INTERESTED ...

...IN YOU!!!
DOKA (KAPOW)
...UM.
ARE YOU OKAY ...?
...... YEAH ...
ZUN (STOMP)
ZUN
ZUN
WHAT?
HERE... FROM SENSEI.
HE SAID IT'S THE SCHEDULE CHANGES FOR TOMORROW.
HE ASKED ME TO GIVE IT TO THE CLASS REPRESENTA-TIVES.
TAKANASHI-SAN WOULD HAVE WORKED TOO.
....
IT WASN'T EVEN A CONFESSION.

HRRRRNGH...
WE CAME ALL THE WAY OUT HERE 'COS HE WAS RUNNING LATE, AND THIS IS WHAT WE FIND...
A COMPLETELY UNEXPECTED DEVELOPMENT!
......
ドキ DOKI (BADMP)
ドキ DOKI
IT'S TACKY TO SPY ON PEOPLE.
HEY! WHAT THE HECK, TAKA!?
TOO LATE TO SAY THAT, DON'T YOU THINK? YOU'RE ALREADY AN ACCOMPLICE!
HEY, DOES THIS MEAN ...?
THE OTHER DAY...
...WHEN KAI WAS TELLING US ABOUT "HIS FRIEND" WHO WAS IN LOVE WITH A GIRL...
DO YOU THINK IT'S SAFE TO ASSUME THE GIRL...
...IS TAKA-NASHI?
....

...I THINK IT'S FINE.
HE DID SECRETLY NURSE TAKANASHI BACK TO HEALTH...
...WHEN SHE CAUGHT A COLD THE OTHER DAY.
FOR REAL? WHY THE HECK—!?
...DUNNO.
HE JUST HAD ME GO BUY MEDICINE.
BUT HE WAS SUPER SECRETIVE ABOUT IT...
...SO I THINK HE'S PRETTY SERIOUS ABOUT HER.
WE REALLY OUGHT TO JUST STAY OUT OF IT AND LET HIM—
UGH, THAT KAI IS SO HOPELESS!!

HE'S DOING THIS ALL WRONG! THERE'S AN ORDER TO THESE THINGS!
WHO GOES IN FOR A SMOOCH RIGHT OFF THE BAT?
EVERYONE KNOWS YOU GOTTA CONFESS YOUR LOVE FIRST!
IS HE RUSHING THINGS BECAUSE HE'S SO SERIOUS ABOUT HER?
WELL, HE'S USED TO HAVING THE GIRLS COME TO HIM. HE'S NEVER REALLY PURSUED BEFORE.
MAYBE HE DOESN'T KNOW HOW IT WORKS.
...OH...
IT'S IRRITATING, BUT I SEE YOUR POINT.
TCH.
....
HEY.
LET'S ...
... JUST—
WELL, NOW WE HAVE NO CHOICE!

FOR OUR DEAR LITTLE HOPELESS FRIEND...
...IT'S TIME TO ROLL UP OUR SLEEVES AND GET TO WORK!!!
WE'LL DO EVERYTHING WE CAN TO HELP KAI IN HIS ROMANTIC ENDEAVORS!
—
....
SIGH...
HUH? TAKA, WHAT'S WRONG?
YOU'RE NOT INTO IT.
FORGET IT.

GOOD MORNING!
GOOD MOR...
— WHY?
WHY IS THIS HAPPEN-ING?
YOU'LL TAKE ANY WOMAN WHO'S BREATHING!?
I WILL NOT, STUPID.
I MEAN, I WOULD HAVE BEFORE.
IF A CUTE GIRL APPROACHED ME, I WOULD WELCOME HER WITH OPEN ARMS.
BUT NOW...

...IT HAS TO BE YOU—
HMPH!

RIKO-CHAN, WHAT'S WRONG?
NOTHING.
....
....
....
DAMN IT... DAMN IT...
WHY IS THIS HAPPENING—!!!?
OOSHIMA-SAN.
EEK!
TO... T-T-T-TORA-MARU-KUN!!
AH-HA-HA...DID I STARTLE YOU?
SORRY.
TH-THAT'S OKAY. WHAT IS IT?

ARE YOU FREE...
...NEXT SUNDAY?
KIIIN (DING)
KOOON (DONG)
KAAAN (DANG)
R-R-R-R-R-RIKO-CHAAAAAN!!!

KIYO...
...WHAT'S WRONG? WHY ARE YOU FREAKING OUT?
COME ON, LET'S GO HOME.
L-L-LISTEN TO THISSSS!!!
IT'S TORA-MARU-KUN!
HE INVITED ME TO THE AMUSEMENT PARK!!!
HMMM?
WHA—?
YOU CAN'T GO, KIYO!!!
NOT WITH THAT WOMANIZING TEMPLE BOY!!
WHAAA...? BUT HE'S HOT, AND HE SEEMS NICE!
WAIT, TEMPLE BOY??
WHAT ARE YOU TALKING ABOUT !!!?
TURN HIM DOWN!

AWWW! BUT I ALREADY TOLD HIM I'D GO!
YOU IDIOT!
WELL, I...
I'VE NEVER HAD A BOY ASK ME OUT BEFORE. I WAS JUST... SO HAPPY...
I'M REALLY TALL, YOU KNOW?
5'8" TALL
I'VE NEVER BEEN TREATED LIKE A GIRL BEFORE.
URK!
AND I ALREADY TOOK THE TICKETS...
HE GAVE ME FOUR AND SAID I SHOULD INVITE THREE GIRL FRIENDS...
......
....
SO HE BASICALLY TRICKED YOU INTO COORDINATING HIS GROUP DATE...
WHAT WERE YOU THINKING?

OKAY, KIYO.
I'LL GO WITH YOU.
PI (FWIP)
RIKO-CHAN! ♡
~~~~!
FINE. I'LL GO TOO.
PI
I CAN'T LET MY DEAR FRIEND WALK INTO DANGER ALONE, AFTER ALL!!
KAGURA-CHAN! ♡
I KNOW IT'LL BE FUN!
I MEAN, THINK OF THE AMAZING GUYS WE'LL BE WITH!
~~~~

TORAMARU-KUN...
THE CUTE KIRITANI-KUN...
THE COOL AND MYSTERIOUS MISAKI-KUN...
AND...
...ICHINOSE-KUN, THE GIRLS' NUMBER ONE FAVORITE!!!
SEE?
IT'S ALL THE HOTTEST GUYS IN OUR YEAR!!
......
HAAH... SO ICHINOSE IS GONNA BE THERE.
HUH?
OH, NOTHING.
BUT THERE'S ONLY THREE OF US.
WE NEED ONE MORE, DON'T WE?
YEAH, I'M NOT SURE WHAT TO DO.
MAYBE WE—

SU (SHF)
KASHA (SNAP)
!?
MIND IF I....
...INVITE MYSELF AND BECOME THAT ONE MORE MERRIER!?

KAI...
...QUIT LAZING AROUND.
GO TAKE A DUMP, AND GO TO BED!
UUUGH...
KAI-KUN, WHY YOU SAD?
ARE YOU SICK?
....
...YEAH.
GUESS I AM.
YOU COULD SAY THAT.

I'VE...
...BEEN DUMPED...
...HAVEN'T I...?
WOW, I THINK THIS IS THE FIRST TIME I'VE EVER BEEN REJECTED.
I SERIOUSLY HAVE NO IDEA WHAT TO DO...
I MEAN, FIRST OF ALL...
...IT'S THE FIRST TIME I'VE EVER REALLY LIKED SOMEONE.
WHY DID IT HAVE TO BE HER?
WHY DID I HAVE TO DO THAT—?

AAAAARRRRGH!
GON (BANG)
MOM-MY!
KAI-KUN SAYS HE'S SICK!
AH?
THEN YOU REALLY SHOULD GO TO BED!
PIRON (BING)
LINE
I got some tickets to the amusement park from a danka family.
Meet up at Waku-Waku Land at 10am tomorrow.
Tora
Roger!
Mikki
...Okay.
Taka
WHA—!?
A THEME PARK WITH A BUNCH OF GUYS!?
ARE THEY INSANE ...?

Taka
...Okay.
Got it.
...WELL... MAYBE IT'LL BE A NICE CHANGE.
I DON'T THINK I WANT ANYTHING TO DO WITH GIRLS FOR A WHILE.
I'M JUST NOT IN THE MOOD.

STUPID, ANNOYING TAKANASHI.
GO AHEAD AND STAY STUCK ON YOUR STUPID ONE-SIDED CRUSH.
I DON'T CARE.

KAI—! OVER HERE!
HEY. MORNING.
YOU HARDLY EVER TAG ALONG ON STUFF LIKE THIS, TAKA.
YOU USUALLY SAY IT'S NOT WORTH THE EFFORT.
......
I TOLD THEM TO LEAVE IT ALONE...
WHAT?
NOTH-ING.
AND YOU, TORA.
WHY WOULD YOU INVITE US HERE INSTEAD OF GIRLS?
WHO SAID ANYTHING ABOUT NO GIRLS?
HUH?
TORAMARU-KUUUN!

THANKS FOR INVITING US TODAY!
HEY, GOOD MORNING!
!?

WAIT A...
HEY, WHAT'S WITH THIS!?
THIS? EXACTLY WHAT IT LOOKS LIKE.
WE'RE LUCKY ENOUGH TO GO TO A COED HIGH SCHOOL! WE HAVE TO MAKE THE MOST OF IT!!
THAT'S OUR COVER, ANYWAY.
"OPERATION—HELP OUR DEAR STUPID FRIEND WITH HIS TRUE LOVE!"
THAT'S WHY WE'RE HERE!!
....
....
SIGHHH.
HUH?
WAIT, KAGURA!?
I DIDN'T KNOW YOU WERE FRIENDS WITH OOSHIMA-SAN.
I'M HERE AS A BODY-GUARD!!
HMPH!
AS LONG AS I LIVE AND BREATHE...
...NO LEWD TEMPLE BOY IS GONNA HAVE HIS WAY WITH MY FRIENDS!!
GOGO (RUMBLE)
GO
GO
GO

WHAT? HOW DO THEY KNOW EACH OTHER?
HE'S THE SON OF THE LOCAL BUDDHIST TEMPLE, AND SHE'S THE DAUGHTER OF THE LOCAL SHINTO SHRINE.
THEY FIGHT LIKE CATS AND DOGS.
WELL, IT'S MORE ONE-SIDED—SHE ABSOLUTELY HATES HIM.
ALWAYS HAS.
OH MAN...
...I REALLY DIDN'T EXPECT TO SEE YOU HERE, KAGURA.
BUT THAT'S OKAY.
CONSIDERING HOW YOU SHARE A CLERICAL BACKGROUND, I CAN SEE WHY SHE DESPISES YOU SO MUCH...I TOTALLY GET IT.
YOU GOT THOSE TICKETS FROM A DANKA GIRL, DIDN'T YOU?
HM?
I DON'T THINK I'VE MET YOU BEFORE.
I KNOW THE OTHERS BECAUSE WE'RE IN THE SAME CLASS.

NICE TO MEET YOU!
I'M AYUMI SHIMURA, MEMBER OF CLASS 1-F AND WRITER FOR THE SCHOOL PAPER!!
I HEARD THE FOUR HOTTEST GUYS IN OUR GRADE WERE ALL GETTING TOGETHER!!
IT STIRRED MY RE-PORTER'S SOUL!!
I KNOW IT'S PRESUMP-TUOUS, BUT I TOOK THE LIBERTY OF NOMINATING MYSELF TO JOIN THE PARTY!!
HA HA HA
HA HA!
CALL IT WHAT IT IS— YOU WERE EAVESDROP-PING.
IT WAS A SURPRISE, BUT A GOOD ONE!
WE WERE SHORT ONE PERSON!
I'M SO RELIEVED TO HEAR YOU SAY THAT! THANK YOU!!
HA HA HA!

WELL, YOU ALL JUST HAVE FUN! THINK OF ME AS YOUR PHOTOGRAPHER!
LEAVE THE PICTURE TAKING TO ME!
WHAT ARE YOU SAYING?
SINCE YOU'RE HERE, YOU SHOULD HAVE FUN WITH US!
I CAN TAKE SOME PICTURES TOO.
RIKO-KUN!!
KYUN (TWANG)
きゅん
YOU'RE SO AWESOME, RIKO-CHAN!
WELL, IF I'M HONEST !!
I DID WANT TO WRITE A REPORT ON THE HOT GUYS, OF COURSE...
...BUT I ADORE CUTE GIRLS TOO!!!
ESPE-CIALLY YOU, RIKO-KUN!
I'VE HEARD STORIES OF YOUR GALLANTRY FOR AGES! I'VE SECRETLY HAD MY EYE ON YOU!!
THAT'S WHY I WAS SPYING IN THE FIRST PLACE!!
THAT'S OUR RIKO-CHAN!
YOU ARE SUCH A BIG PERSON IN SUCH A LITTLE PACKAGE!!
......

THESE GIRLS ARE A HANDFUL.
HMM...
WE CAN'T LET THEM BEAT US!!
IT'S A COMPE-TITION?
WELL.
PON (PAT)
THERE YOU HAVE IT, KAI.
LET'S ALL HAVE FUN TODAY!
BACHIIIN (WINK)
HUH...?
H... HAVE FUN?

BUT TAKANASHI IS COM-PLETELY IGNORING ME...

TSUUUN (FLIP)
GAAAN (SHOCK)
...AND YOU...
COME ON, LET'S GO IN.
SUTA (STEP)
SUTA
...YOU EXPECT ME...
...TO "HAVE FUN"!? HOW—!?

Tarou Toramaru
The playboy temple heir
Takaya Misaki
Wants as hassle-free a life as possible
Miki Kiritani
Biggest concern is he's often mistaken for a girl
SO WHEN YOU GET DOWN TO IT...
...THIS IS A DATE, RIGHT?

Kagura Tatsunami
The neat-freak shrine heiress
BATTERY CHARGED, PLENTY OF MEMORY!
Ayumi Shimura
The impulsive rookie reporter
Kiyo Ooshima
The laid-back girly girl who's most worried about how tall she is

Kai Ichinose
The school's most popular guy, currently troubled by his first love
Riko Takanashi
A small, gutsy girl whose one-sided love keeps growing

WITH A RATHER STRANGE MIXTURE OF CHAR-ACTERS...
...THE AMUSE-MENT PARK DATE IS ABOUT TO BEGIN—

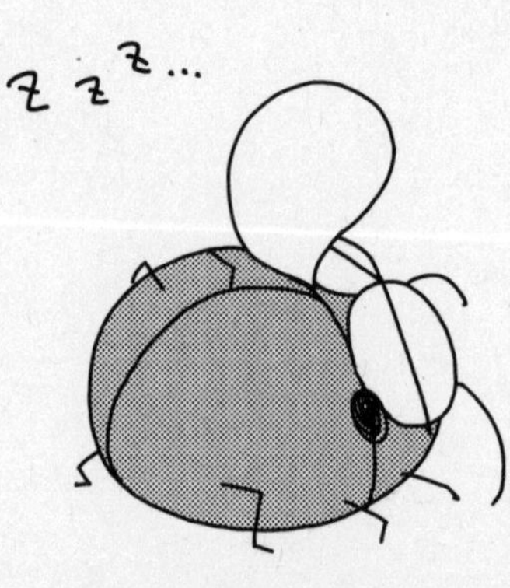
z z z...

YOUR HEART LEAPS, AND YOU'RE SO HAPPY YOU CAN'T STAND STILL.
THAT'S WHAT I THOUGHT LOVE WAS LIKE.

CHAPTER 6

Z
Z
Z... Gasp!
I got an incredibly wonderful gift! Hurry to the next bonus page!!

THIS IS WEIRD.
IF I RECALL CORRECTLY ...
...IT'S SUPPOSED TO BE FUN TO GO TO AN AMUSEMENT PARK WITH GIRLS.
KASHA (SNAP) カシャ
KASHA カシャ
KASHA カシャ
WHAT SHOULD WE GO ON FIRST?

hatsu haru

IT WAS NEVER, EVER SUPPOSED TO MAKE ME FEEL LIKE THIS.
DOKI (BADMP)
ドキドキ
DOKI
HARA (JITTER)
ハラハラ
HARA
I WASN'T THINKING ON THAT CAMPING TRIP. I SHOULDN'T HAVE DONE THAT.
BUT I DID, AND SHE WENT BALLISTIC.

SHE'S BEEN IGNORING ME EVER SINCE...
...AND NOW I'M HERE WITH HER... THIS IS WORSE THAN TORTURE.
MAAAN— I WANNA GO HOME ...!!
I'VE NEVER FELT THIS WAY AT AN AMUSEMENT PARK...
BIKU (WINCE)
!

UGH...
WHY ARE YOU SO JUMPY?
UH!?
I-I AM NOT JUMPY!!
DOKII (BADMP)
I HAVE NO IDEA WHAT YOU'RE TALKING ABOUT!!
IF YOU'RE WORRIED ABOUT THE OTHER DAY, I'M OVER IT.
MY FRIENDS ARE ALL HERE TO HAVE FUN, AND I DON'T WANT TO RUIN THE MOOD.
SO I'LL DO YOU A FAVOR AND FORGET THE WHOLE THING. IT'LL BE LIKE ALMOST GETTING BIT BY A DOG.

COME ON.
WE BETTER GO.
THEY'RE GOING WITHOUT US!
—A...
RIKO-CHAN! SIT NEXT TO ME ON THE ROLLER COASTER!
OKAY, OKAY.
カシャ
KASHA (SNAP)
DOG.
A DOG ...!?
ME!?

WHAT'S THAT SUPPOSED TO MEAN?
SO TAKANASHI DOESN'T EVEN SEE ME AS A MAN...
AAAAAH!
...AM I NOT EVEN HUMAN TO HER!?
WELCOME BACK!
...
THAT WAS SO SCARY!
ARE YOU OKAY?
URP...!
HA HA HA!
AAAAAH!!
DON'T...
...SPIN IT SO FAST.
THAT... THAT LITTLE...!
GO (RUMBLE)
GO
GO
GO
GO

JUST YOU WATCH.
I'LL SHOW YOU JUST HOW MUCH OF A MAN I CAN BE!!!
HMMMM.
IS IT ME, OR ARE THE SEATING ARRANGEMENTS KINDA OFF-BALANCE?
I'M NOT ENJOYING THEM AT ALL.
HUH?
BUT THERE'S NOT MUCH WE CAN DO.

THE GIRLS ARE ALL SUPER CLOSE.
AND MORE THAN ANY-THING...
...WE CAN'T GET CLOSE TO THEM WITH THAT GUARDIAN SPIRIT IN THE WAY.
RIKO-CHAN! WHAT DO YOU WANT TO TRY NEXT?
KASHA (SNAP)
KASHA
I WILL PROTECT MY FRIENDS' VIRTUE!!
ALL RIGHT, YOU GOT ME.
THAT KAGURA.
IT'S YOUR FAULT, YOU KNOW.
THAT SHE'S LIKE THAT.
OUR GOAL TODAY IS SUP-POSED TO BE GETTING KAI AND TAKANASHI TOGETHER.
EVEN TAKA'S LOOKING AT US LIKE, "WHAT WAS THE POINT?"
BUTSU (MUTTER)
BUTSU
BUTSU
......
HMMM. PERSONALLY, I WAS THINKING I'D LIKE TO GO FOR SHIMURA-SAN.
SHE'S GOT A PRETTY NICE FIGURE.
BUT FINE! I'LL DO SOMETHING!
Haunted House
ENTRANCE

HUH?
WHEN YOU GO THROUGH A HAUNTED HOUSE...
...THE PROPER WAY IS IN BOY-GIRL PAIRS, RIGHT?
...... OH.
UM, GUYS...
AAAND ...
...THAT BEING THE CAAASE—
LET'S GO, KAGURA!
WHA—!?
ME!?
OH!
READY TO GO, OOSHIMA!!?
DOKI (BADMP)
HUH !?
O-OKAY!

...WELL.
WANNA GO?
OH!
ARE YOU SURE YOU WANT TO GO WITH ME?
I'M HONORED TO BE CHOSEN BY SUCH A HOT GUY!!
LET'S DO IT!
....
....

SO I GUESS THIS MEANS...
Y...
...WE'RE STUCK TOGETHER.
DOKI (BADMP)
ドキッ
YEAH...
WHAT ARE YOU WAITING FOR?
LET'S GO.
...Y—
YEAH!
ヒュー
HYUUU (WHOOOOSH)
DORO (OOZE)
ドロ
DORO
ドロ
DORO
ドロ
DORO
ドロ

THEY'VE GOT EVERYTHING. THIS IS PRETTY COOL.
Y...
HMM, IT'S LIKE A COMBINATION OF SHINTO AND BUDDHISM, BUT ALSO EASTERN AND WESTERN INFLUENCES.
YEAH, SURE...
THE CLERICS
LABEL: EVIL SPIRITS BEGONE
HUH? KAGURA, ARE YOU ACTUALLY SCARED?
D—
DON'T BE STUPID!!!
I-I-I-I-I COME FROM A LONG LINE OF ANCIENT AND HONORABLE SHINTO PRIESTS!
I-I-I-I WOULD NEVER BE SCARED OF THESE SHODDY FAKES!!!
DON'T PUT ME ON YOUR LEVEL, YOU IRRESPONSIBLE, FLASHY MONK!!
WOW, YOU ARE SO HOPE-LESS.

YOU'VE ALWAYS PUT ON A TOUGH-GUY ACT, HUH?
COME ON.
BA (FWIP)
ばっ
WHA—
WH-WH-WH-WHAT ARE YOU DOING?
YOU'LL GET ME PREG-NANT !!!

WHAT? HA-HA-HA.
BUT AS A JOKE, IT'S KIND OF A STRETCH.
AS A MAN, I AM EXTREMELY HONORED THAT YOU WOULD THINK SO HIGHLY OF MY VIRILITY.
....
TH-THAT WAS A JOKE, RIGHT?
YOU DON'T REALLY THINK YOU CAN MAKE A BABY JUST BY HOLDING HANDS, DO YOU?
OF COURSE IT WAS!
IT WAS JUST A METAPHOR TO DESCRIBE THE FILTHY FEELING OF TOUCHING YOUR PROMISCUOUS HAND!!
WHEW. THAT'S A RELIEF.
BUT SERIOUSLY, YOU DON'T HAVE TO WORRY.
I WILL ABSOLUTELY NEVER, EVER SEE YOU THAT WAY, KAGURA.

COME ON, LET'S GO.
....
BA (FWIP)
バッ
HEY! KAGURA!
I DON'T NEED YOU.
ずんずん
ZUN... (TROMP)
ZUN
I'LL BE FINE ON MY OWN!
BON (POP)
EEK!
GOOD GRIEF.

ヒュー
HYUUU (WHOOSH)
ド口 DORO (OOZE)
ド口 DORO
ド口… DORO
IT...IT'S GOT THE RIGHT ATMOSPHERE, HUH...?
ドキ DOKI (BADMP)
ドキ DOKI
ビク BIKU (WINCE)
ビク BIKU
Y... YEAH...
THE PURE ONES
....
....
I KNOW IT JUST KIND OF HAPPENED ...
...BUT IT SURE MAKES ME NERVOUS, BEING ALONE IN THE DARK WITH A GIRL...
ドキ DOKI
ドキ DOKI
KIRI-TANI-KUN...
I WONDER WHY HE CHOSE ME.
COULD... COULD IT BE HE...?
ドキ DOKI
ドキ DOKI

BUT IF I HAD TO DO THIS ANYWAY, I WISH I COULD HAVE GONE WITH A SMALLER GIRL.
OOSHIMA'S PRETTY HUGE.
I DON'T WANNA BE SEEN NEXT TO HER...
WHAT DO I DO IF HE DOES?
I DON'T THINK I LIKE THIS.
I WANT A GUY WHO'S TALLER THAN ME...
BON (POOF)
SHAA (HISSS)
GYAAAAAAAAAHH!
KYAAAAAAAAAAHH!
KYAAAAAAAAAAHH!
K-YAAAAAH!
....
...C...CALM DOWN!
SHUUU (FSHHH)
DO (THMP)
DO
EEEEK!
NNNGH!

I'M SCARED.
IT...IT'S OKAY!
IT'S NOT REAL!
B... BUT...!
I...I'LL HOLD YOUR HAND!!
THEN IT WON'T BE SO SCARY, RIGHT!?

....
RIGHT...
......
OOSHIMA IS SURPRISINGLY CUTE...
DOKI (BADMP)
DOKI
HE MIGHT BE SMALL...BUT KIRITANI-KUN IS ACTUALLY PRETTY MANLY.
BAA (WHOOSH)
EEK!
AAAAHH!

ヒューー
HYUUU (WHOOOSH)
ドロドロ
DORO DORO (OOZE)
WOW! THE OUTSIDE WAS A JAPANESE STYLE, BUT ON THE INSIDE, THEY'VE GOT WESTERN STUFF TOO!
IN A WAY, THE BLEND IS VERY JAPANESE.
IS THAT A WAX STATUE? IT'S SO REALISTIC!
DO YOU THINK THE PEOPLE PLAYING GHOSTS PLAY GHOSTS EVERY DAY?
OR DO THEY SWITCH OUT?
... DUNNO.
THE REALISTS
SO YOU'RE OKAY WITH THIS KIND OF STUFF, MISAKI-KUN?
YEAH, PRETTY MUCH.
I'M NOT SCARED, ANYWAY.
HMM, HMM. "OKAY WITH HORROR."
END QUOTE.
SARA (WRITE)
SARA
...
SO WHAT GENRE OF MOVIES DO YOU LIKE?
ACTION? COMEDY?
WHAT ARE YOUR FAVORITE FOODS?
...
DO YOU HAVE ANY HOBBIES!?

...WHAT ARE YOU DOING?
WHAT AM I DOING? HELLO!!
IT'S AN INTERVIEW!!
HOW OFTEN AM I GONNA GET TO BE ALONE WITH THE SCHOOL'S NUMBER ONE MYSTERIOUS COOL BEAUTY!!?
BISHI (FWIP)
AS A WRITER FOR THE SCHOOL PAPER, I CAN'T LET THIS OPPORTUNITY PASS ME BY!!
...
WHAT THE...
SO? WHAT'S YOUR ANSWER TO MY LAST QUESTION!?
......NONE IN PARTICULAR.
HMMM, IS THAT SO!
HAVE YOU BEEN FRIENDS WITH ICHINOSE-KUN AND THE OTHERS LONG?
...KAI AND I GO WAY BACK.
HOW LONG?
SINCE GRADE SCHOOL.
MM-HM, MM-HM!

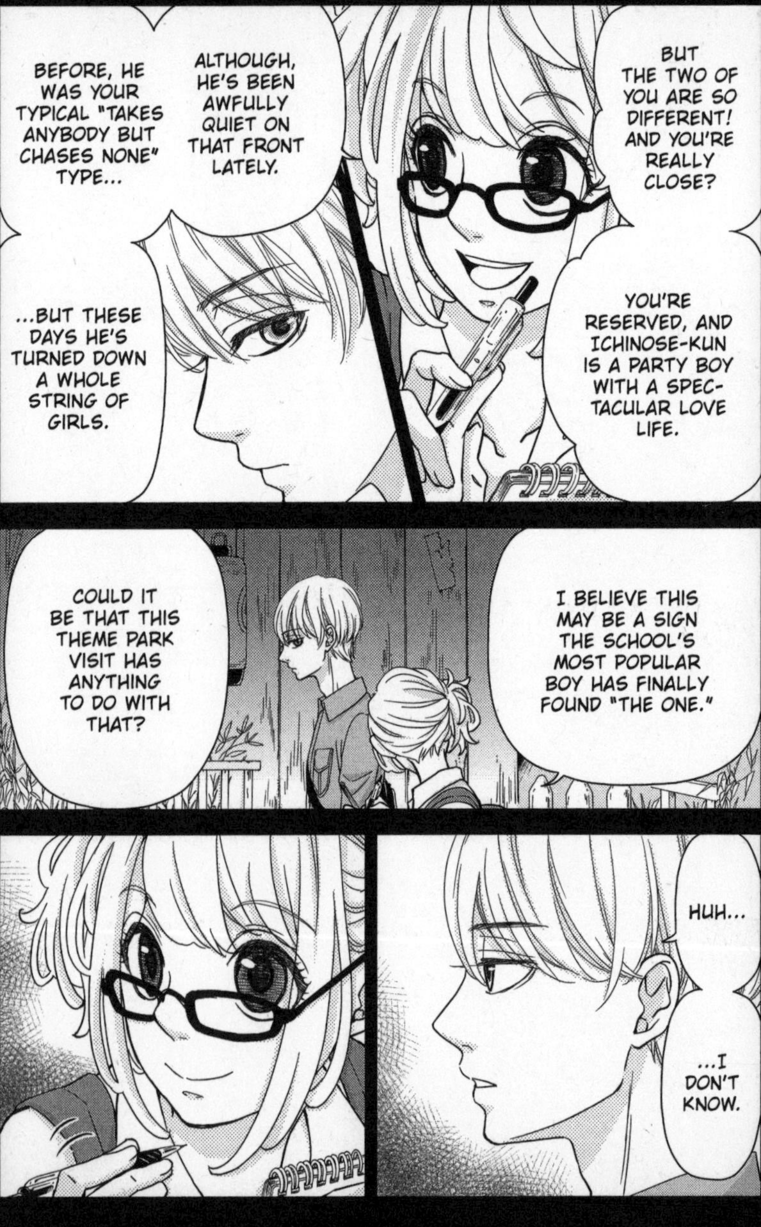
BUT THE TWO OF YOU ARE SO DIFFERENT! AND YOU'RE REALLY CLOSE?
YOU'RE RESERVED, AND ICHINOSE-KUN IS A PARTY BOY WITH A SPEC-TACULAR LOVE LIFE.
ALTHOUGH, HE'S BEEN AWFULLY QUIET ON THAT FRONT LATELY.
BEFORE, HE WAS YOUR TYPICAL "TAKES ANYBODY BUT CHASES NONE" TYPE...
...BUT THESE DAYS HE'S TURNED DOWN A WHOLE STRING OF GIRLS.
I BELIEVE THIS MAY BE A SIGN THE SCHOOL'S MOST POPULAR BOY HAS FINALLY FOUND "THE ONE."
COULD IT BE THAT THIS THEME PARK VISIT HAS ANYTHING TO DO WITH THAT?
HUH...
...I DON'T KNOW.

I SEE!
ANYWAY.
THEN I GUESS I'LL JUST HAVE TO KEEP FOLLOWING THIS LEAD THE SLOW AND STEADY WAY!
PATAN (SHUT)
パタン
IT'S REALLY SOMETHING THAT A GOLDEN PAIR OF HOTTIES LIKE YOU TWO HAVE BEEN TOGETHER FOR SO MANY YEARS!!
ICHINOSE-KUN'S POPULARITY IS SO OVERWHELMING, IT'S EASY FOR YOU TO BE HIDDEN IN HIS SHADOW...
...BUT YOU HAVE QUITE A FOLLOWING YOURSELF, YOU KNOW.
ICHINOSE-KUN HAS A LOT OF CASUAL, TREND-FOLLOWER TYPES AS FANS...
...WHILE THOSE INTERESTED IN YOU STAY IN THE DARK WITH DEEP, DEVOTED FEELINGS.
SO IT'S POSSIBLE YOU'RE EVEN MORE POPULAR THAN HE IS!
—THAT'S WHAT MAKES IT SO STRANGE.

NO MATTER HOW DEEP I DIG...
...I CAN'T FIND A SINGLE LOVE STORY STARRING YOU.
—DOES THIS MEAN...
...YOU HAVE A SECRET LOVE YOURSELF?

GYAAAAAAHH!
KYAAAAAAHH!
!!
THAT'S A SURPRISE.
THERE ARE ACTUALLY PEOPLE SCARED BY THIS STUFF!
AAAAAAH!
....
...YOU'LL DROP YOUR PEN.
WHY DON'T YOU PUT IT AWAY?
GOOD IDEA!
THIS INTERVIEW IS OVER.
I'LL JUST SHUT UP AND ENJOY THE HAUNTED HOUSE TO THE FULLEST.
BA (FIP)
HEY, THANKS FOR YOUR HARD WORK!
......

ヒュ〜〜〜
HYUUU (WHOOSH)
DORO (OOZE)
ドロ
DORO
ドロ
DORO
ドロ
THE THEME IN HERE IS ALL OVER THE PLACE.
... YEAH ...
THE CLASS REPRESENTATIVES
KURU (TURN)
くるっ
SHAKI (JOLT)
シャキッ
?
WHAT ARE YOU DOING? YOU NEED TO KEEP UP.
KIRI (FLIP)
キリッ
SH-SHUT UP! JUST LEAVE ME ALONE!

BON (POOF)
EEP!
BA (FLINCH)
SHUUU (FSHHH)
......ICHINOSE...
...ARE YOU SCARED?
D-
DON'T BE STUPID!
LIKE HELL I'M SCARED!

WH...WHAT ABOUT YOU? AREN'T YOU SCARED?
NOT REALLY.
......
THAT CASUAL LOOK ON HER FACE.
......
COULD ANYONE BE LESS CUTE!?
SERIOUSLY, IS SHE EVEN FEMALE!!!?
YOU CAN BE HONEST.
I TOLD YOU I'M NOT SCAR—!
BA (BOO)
AAARRGH!
ACK!
......

OH NO.
SHE'S GONNA KILL ME...!!!
THIS TIME FOR SURE!
KYU (TUG)
!?
WHA...? A BLIND-FOLD!?
IS THIS SOME NEW KIND OF PUNISH-MENT!!?
AIEEEEEEE!
THERE.

IF YOU CAN'T SEE THEM, THEY WON'T SCARE YOU, RIGHT?
COME ON, LET'S GO!
IT'S OKAY!
I PROMISE I'LL GET YOU TO THE EXIT.
TAKANASHI ...! ...

YOU'RE SUCH A STUD ......!!!
きゅきゅ〜ん
KYU-KYUUN (TWANG)
OKAY, OKAY.
EXCUSE US!
FEELING BETTER?
...... YEAH...

FACT: BIG SISTERS EXIST TO TRAUMATIZE THEIR KID BROTHERS.

YOUR SISTER IS HILARIOUS!
AH HA HA HA HA!
SHUT UP.
IT'S NOT FUNNY TO ME.
SHE SCARRED ME FOR LIFE.
SORRY, SORRY.
BUT IT'S CUTE TO HAVE A WEAKNESS.
GUYS DON'T WANNA BE CUTE.
OKAY, OKAY.
I'LL STOP.
ANYWAY, WHERE DO YOU THINK EVERYBODY WENT?
………………

TAKA-NASHI.
HMM?
LEAVE ME HERE AND GO FIND EVERYONE ELSE.
I BET YOU'RE BORED SITTING AROUND.
IF YOU CAN TALK SO MUCH...
...YOU MUST BE FEELING A LOT BETTER!
SUKKU (STAND)
すっく
I'LL BUY US SOMETHING TO DRINK.
WHAT DO YOU WANT?

POCARI.
YOU GOT IT!
TAKANASHI...
...THANKS.

WHAT AM I DOING?

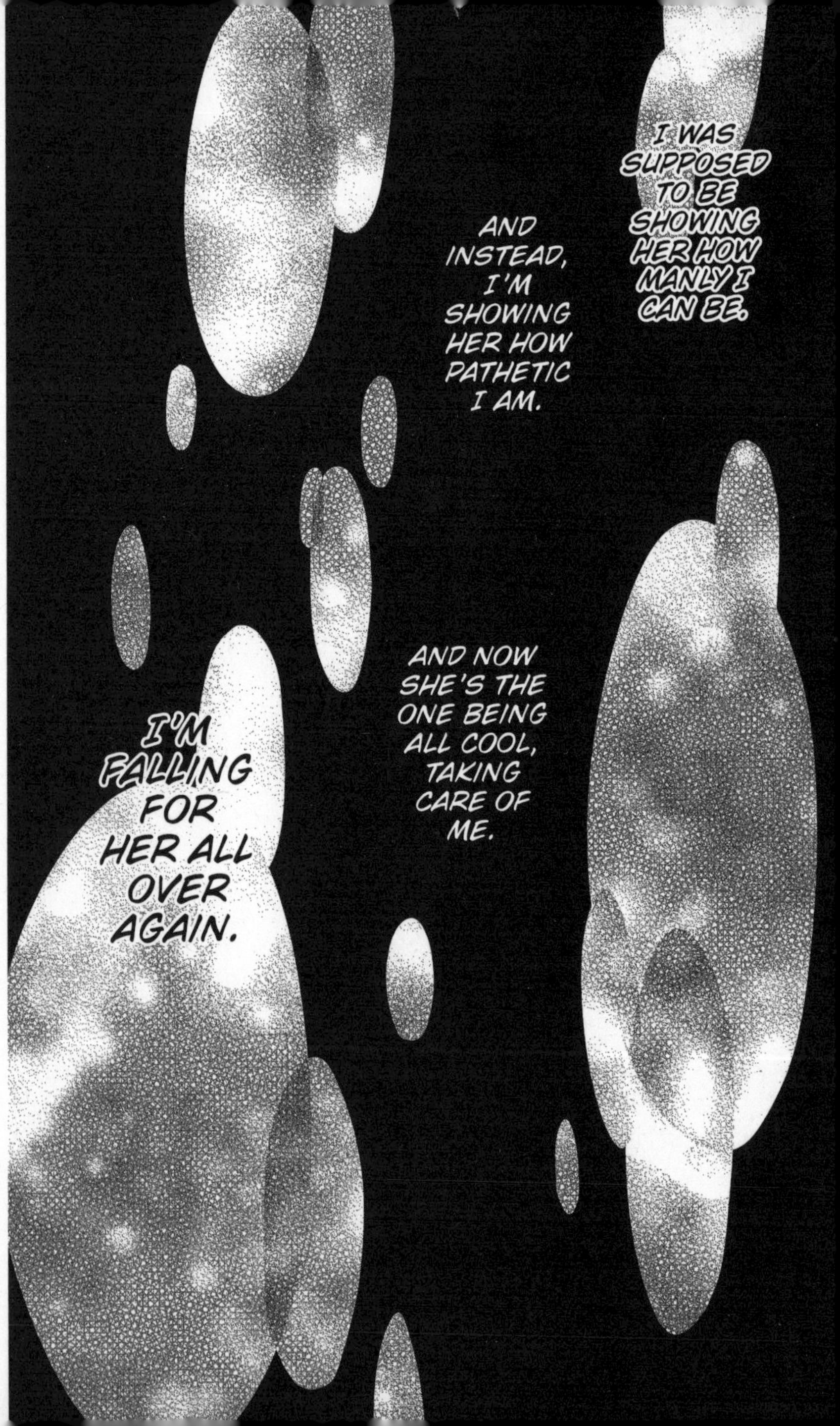
I WAS SUPPOSED TO BE SHOWING HER HOW MANLY I CAN BE.
AND INSTEAD, I'M SHOWING HER HOW PATHETIC I AM.
AND NOW SHE'S THE ONE BEING ALL COOL, TAKING CARE OF ME.
I'M FALLING FOR HER ALL OVER AGAIN.

DAMN IT.
HAVE I ALWAYS BEEN SUCH A LOSER?
WHY DO I ALWAYS END UP LIKE THIS IN FRONT OF HER?
—WHY...

...DOES SHE HAVE TO BE INTO ANOTHER GUY?
GEH!
SUWA!?
AM I SO DISGUSTED I'M HALLUCI-NATING!!?

GOSHI (RUB)
ごし
GOSHI
ごし
NO, HE'S REAL!?
HE'S REALLY HERE!!
HERE!!
—WAIT...

WHO'S THAT WITH HIM!?

CHAPTER 7

Kai's Romantic Endeavors Support Group
Tora
Let's just leave Kai and Takanashi alone for now.
2:05PM
Tora
Stay split up, guys.
2:06PM
Mikki
Roger that! (^o^)/ And we'll enjoy the park while we're at it! (^_^)b
2:07PM
...
SO WHERE IS EVERYBODY?

hatsu haru

APPARENTLY THEY'RE ALL OFF DOING THEIR OWN THING.
WE'LL RUN INTO THEM SOON ENOUGH.
HMMM. I SEE.
HERE! YOUR ICED TEA!
KAI...
I WONDER IF HE MADE IT THROUGH THE HAUNTED HOUSE...
HE CAN'T STAND THAT STUFF...
KASHA (FLASH)
!?
OH, SORRY.
YOU JUST LOOKED SO SEXY.
I COULDN'T HELP IT.
MY REPORTER'S BLOOD IS ON FIRE.
......
WAIT, WAIT, WAIT.
WAAAIT...

WHAT IS SUWA DOING HERE—!!?
AND WHO'S THAT WITH HIM—!!!?
DIDN'T YOU TELL ME...
GIRLS AREN'T INTO ME AT ALL.
...JUST THE OTHER DAY!!!?
ARE YOU A LIAR!?
RIGHT. SO NOW YOU'RE GONNA TELL ME, "OH, SHE'S MY SISTER"!
IS THAT HOW IT IS!?

THE HELL IT ISSS!!
A THEME PARK WITH HIS SISTER?
NOT A CHANCE!
ICHI-NOSE?
WHAT ARE YOU FLAILING AROUND FOR?
ARE YOU FEELING BETTER?
!!!
?
HERE'S YOUR DRINK.
—...!

GUI (YANK)
HEY!
WHAT'S GOTTEN INTO YOU!?
JUST COME WITH ME!
—
WHAT'S WRONG?
NOTHING, JUST...
I THOUGHT I HEARD A FAMILIAR VOICE...
CAN: POCARI SWEAT
OKAY!
......
GON (KLONG)
OW!

WHAT ARE YOU DOING!?
I SHOULD BE ASKING YOU THAT!
WHAT'S GOING ON?
DOES THIS MEAN YOU'RE ALL BETTER NOW?
TAKE YOUR DRINK.
...YEAH.
I GUESS SO.
PUSHI (PSHH)
—I WONDER ...
BOTTLE: ORONAMIN C DRINK
...IF TAKANASHI KNOWS...
...SUWA HAS A GIRL-FRIEND.
YOU SURE YOU'RE OKAY?

NO!!!
OF COURSE SHE DOESN'T KNOW!!
IF SHE KNEW, SHE WOULDN'T INSIST ON HOLDING ON TO HER STUPID CRUSH.
ER...
WAAAAUGH!!!
Hey!
W-w-we should quit wasting time around here...
...and go on a ride!!
GOTTA MAKE THE MOST OF THOSE TICKETS!
...WHY ARE YOU WHISPER-ING?
WAIT.

WHAT DO YOU WANNA RIDE?
THAT WAY.
SOME-THING OVER THERE.
WHAT AM I DOING?
THERE'S NO REASON FOR ME TO PUT SO MUCH EFFORT INTO AVOIDING SUWA.
DOES IT MATTER IF SHE FINDS OUT HE HAS A GIRL?
IF SHE DOES...
...TAKANASHI WILL GIVE UP ON HIM.
AND THEN I COULD ...

YEAH!! THERE'S NO REASON I SHOULD COVER FOR HIM!!
THIS'LL MAKES THINGS BETTER FOR ME!
SHOVE REALITY IN HER FACE...
...AND SAY GOOD-BYE TO THAT STUPID CRUSH ONCE AND FOR ALL!!!
BUT...

...THEN TAKANASHI WOULD—

DAN
(BAM)
......UH.

THAT WAS CLOSE!!!
DO (THMP)
DO
QUIT WANDERING AROUND, DAMMIT!
DO
DO
HAH!
HEY, DIDN'T I JUST DECIDE...
...THAT I WOULDN'T HIDE THEM—
HM?
GO (RUMBLE)
GO
GO
GO
GO
GO
PAKI (WHAP)
HRK!
YOOOUUUU LITTTLLLE...

I THOUGHT YOU'D BEEN ACTING KIND OF WEIRD...
YOU'VE REALLY LOST IT, HAVEN'T YOU!!?
HUH!? WHAT'RE YOU TALKING ABOUT?
WHY'D YOU RANDOMLY PIN ME ON THE WALL!?
IF YOU'RE GONNA CHASE A GIRL, PICK SOMEBODY CUTER, STUPID!!!
WHA—!?
WHAT KIND OF CRAZY, SELF-CONSCIOUS NONSENSE—!?
OF COURSE I LIKE 'EM CUTE, YOU STUPID PIECE OF—!

YOU'D GO AFTER A MOVING SKIRT, HUH? ARE YOU PERPETUALLY IN HEAT?
WHAT!?
I WOULD IN THE PAST!
BUT BECAUSE OF YOU, NOW I CAN'T APPRECIATE OTHER GIRLS! HOW ARE YOU GONNA MAKE IT UP TO ME!?
AND DO YOU THINK ALL GIRLS LIKE BEING PINNED TO WALLS!?
YOU READ TOO MUCH SHOUJO MANGA!!!
I DON'T READ THAT STUFF!!!
I'M A DUDE!
UGH, THIS WOMAN—
—OH?

RIKO?
WE'VE BEEN SPOTTED !!!
HUH?
WAIT A MINUTE—

THEY KNOW EACH OTHER?
...AKEMI-ONEECHAN.
IT IS YOU, RIKO.
WHAT'S THIS? ARE YOU ON A DATE TOO?
"ONEE-CHAN"!?
SIS-TERS !?
NO WAY.
WE GOT SPLIT UP FROM OUR FRIENDS.
THAT'S A BOY FROM MY CLASS.
BUT THAT LOOKED LIKE A PRETTY SERIOUS WALL-PIN BACK THERE.
JI (GLANCE)
HE'S SUPER HOT.
NICE WORK.
IT'S NOT LIKE THAT!!

LET'S GO, SATOSHI.
WE SHOULDN'T BE BOTHERING THE KIDDOS.
UH, RIGHT.
SEE YOU LATER, RIKO-CHAN. ICHINOSE-KUN.
HEY—!
IT'S NOT WHAT YOU THINK!!
OH.
THAT REMINDS ME, RIKO.
SATOSHI'S UNCLE SAYS HE CAUGHT A HORSE MACKEREL.
JUST GOT A TEXT.
SO WE'LL BE MAKING SASHIMI AT SATOSHI'S HOUSE LATER TODAY.
YOU SHOULD COME JOIN US.
BUT...
...I DON'T KNOW WHAT TIME I'LL BE GETTING HOME TONIGHT.

DON'T STAY OUT TOO LATE. IT'S NOT SAFE.
...I'LL BE FINE.
I'M NOT A CHILD ANYMORE.
ぽん PON (PAT)
ぽん PON
YES YOU ARE.

WELL, SEE YOU AT SCHOOL, ICHINOSE-KUN.
RIKO-CHAN...
...I'LL SEE YOU LATER.
...YEAH.

OKAY! WHAT SHOULD WE GO ON NEXT?
WE'VE COVERED A LOT OF GROUND.
HEY!!!
WHEN ARE WE GOING TO MEET UP WITH EVERYBODY ELSE!?
CAW!
CAW!
THE SUN IS GOING DOWN!!
WHO CARES ABOUT THEM?
THEY'RE ALL OUT THERE HAVING FUN.
I AM NOT HAVING THE LEAST BIT OF FUN!!!
WHY AM I STUCK WITH YOU!!?
AAGH!
WHEN I THINK HOW ONE OF MY DEAR FRIENDS MIGHT BE FALLING PREY TO ONE OF YOU STARVING WOLVES' VENOMOUS FANGS AS WE SPEAK...
I'M SO WORRIED, I FEEL LIKE MY HEART IS GOING TO SHATTER!!
AAAAAHHH!

THEY'LL BE FINE.
THEY'RE PROBABLY ALL GETTING CHUMMY ON THE FERRIS WHEEL.
COME ON, LET'S GO!
THAT'S NOT FINE!!!
THAT'S AN ENCLOSED SPACE! THAT'S SUPER DANGEROUS!!!
KIYO! SHIMURA-SAN! RIKOOOO!!!

THE AIR FEELS HEAVY.
I'M NOT GOOD WITH THIS KIND OF THING.
—I...
I THOUGHT YOU WERE AN ONLY CHILD.
FOR SOME REA-SON.
WHAT?
THAT WOMAN... SHE WAS YOUR SISTER, RIGHT?
OH.
NO, SHE'S NOT.
THAT'S SUWA-SENSEI'S GIRLFRIEND.
YEAH. BUT...
...SHE FEELS LIKE A REAL SISTER TO ME.

THOSE TWO...
...HAVE BEEN DATING SINCE FOREVER.
I WAS USUALLY HOME ALONE BECAUSE OF MY MOM'S WORK...
...SO I GUESS THEY'VE ALWAYS WORRIED ABOUT ME.
THEY'D INVITE ME TO DINNER LIKE SHE DID BACK THERE.
THEY'D EVEN TAKE ME ALONG ON THEIR DATES.

SO IT'S LIKE...
...THEY REALLY ARE MY BROTHER AND SISTER.

SHE IS SERIOUSLY...
...SO NOT CUTE.
SHE'S NOT EVEN HAPPY, BUT SHE SMILES LIKE AN IDIOT.
IF SHE WOULD JUST ACT A LITTLE DEPRESSED, I COULD DO SOMETHING TO HELP HER FEEL BETTER.
IF THESE FEELINGS WOULD DESTROY SOMETHING PRECIOUS TO ME...
...I'D RATHER KEEP THEM LOCKED UP FOREVER.

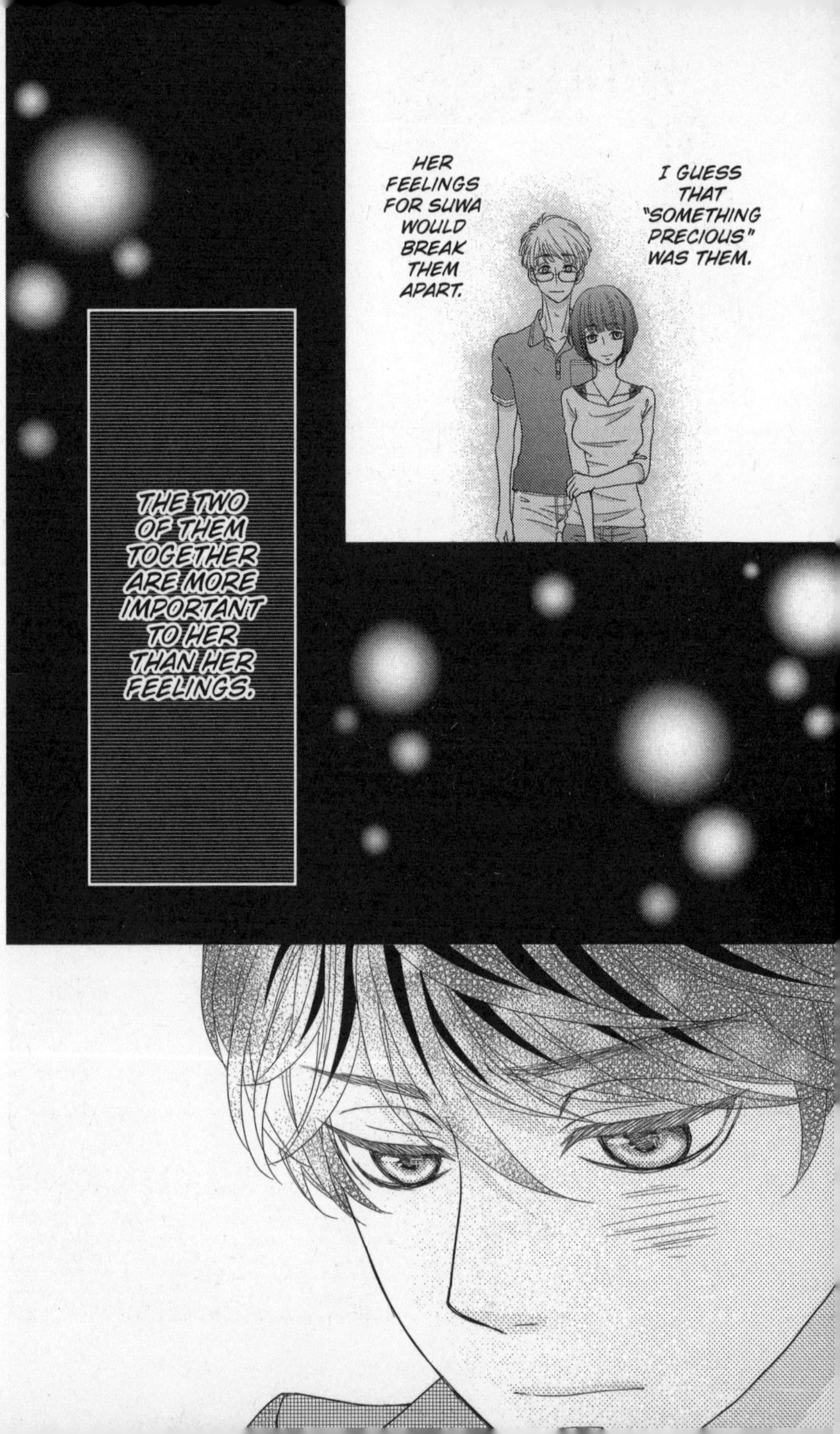
I GUESS THAT "SOMETHING PRECIOUS" WAS THEM.
HER FEELINGS FOR SUWA WOULD BREAK THEM APART.
THE TWO OF THEM TOGETHER ARE MORE IMPORTANT TO HER THAN HER FEELINGS.

HOW STUPID IS SHE?
BUT...
ICHINOSE.
YEAH?
YOU KNEW THE TWO OF THEM WERE HERE, DIDN'T YOU?
AND YOU TRIED TO HIDE IT, BECAUSE YOU THOUGHT SEEING THEM WOULD REALLY HURT ME.
I THOUGHT YOU WERE ACTING STRANGE. NOW I KNOW WHY.
URK!
THAT'S SO STUPID. I ALREADY KNEW.
WHAT DO YOU MEAN STUPID!!!?
LOOK WHO'S TALKING!!
—ICHINOSE.

...THANK YOU.

...HMPH.
SHE SACRIFICES HER OWN FEELINGS...
...FOR THE SAKE OF SOMETHING SHE CARES ABOUT MORE—
I THOUGHT SHE WAS STUPID.

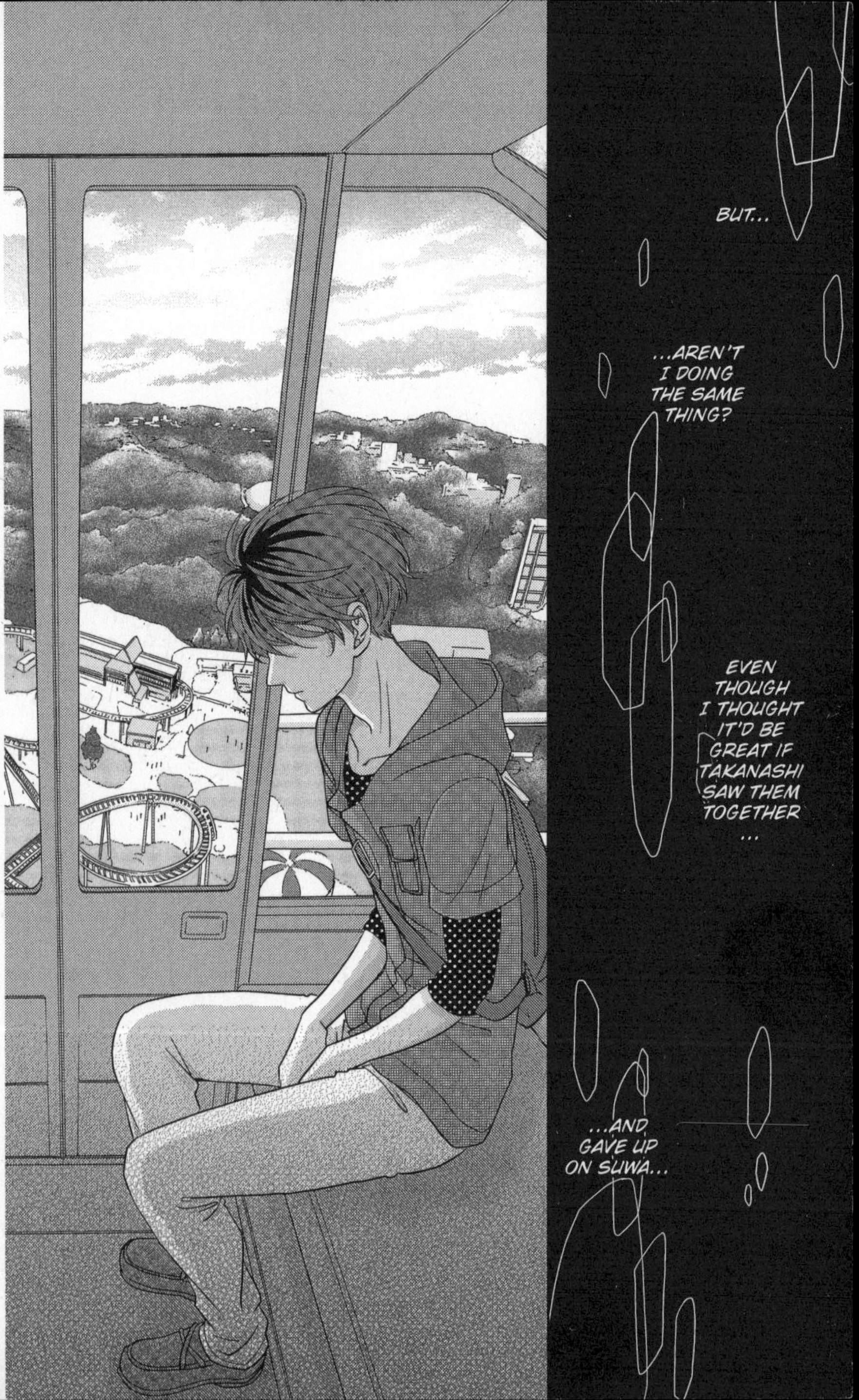
BUT...
...AREN'T I DOING THE SAME THING?
EVEN THOUGH I THOUGHT IT'D BE GREAT IF TAKANASHI SAW THEM TOGETHER...
...AND GAVE UP ON SUWA...

...WHEN I THOUGHT ABOUT HOW SHE'D FEEL, I COULDN'T DO IT.

I WONDER IF FALLING IN LOVE WITH SOMEONE...
...MEANS PUTTING THEIR FEELINGS BEFORE YOUR OWN.

OH!
HEEEY!
THERE YOU ALL ARE!
RIKOO-OOO—!!!
ARE YOU OKAY!?
ICHINOSE-KUN DIDN'T TRY ANYTHING FUNNY, DID HE!?
...HEY.
NO, NO.
YOU WORRY TOO MUCH.

HOW CAN YOU SAY THAT!?
I WAS BESIDE MYSELF WITH WORRY!
RIGHT!?
AWW, BUT I HAD A LOT OF FUN.
YEAH!
IT WAS A GOOD DAY FOR ME TOO! I GOT AN UP-CLOSE-AND-PERSONAL INTERVIEW WITH MISAKI-KUN!!
......
THANKS FOR TAKING PICTURES, AYUMI-CHAN!
OH, IT'S NOTHING!
I GOT LOADS OF GREAT PHOTOS TO USE!!
NOW I JUST HAVE TO PRODUCE SOME HOT-GUY GOSSIP AND SELL IT TO THE GIRLS...
...AND THE PERPETUALLY DRIED-UP FUNDS OF THE SCHOOL PAPER WILL FINALLY SEE SOME RAIN.
こそ…
KOSO (MUTTER)
REALLY? I WANNA SEE.
ピッ
PI (BEEP)
ピッ
PI
WOW, THESE ARE PRETTY GOOD.
YOU THINK SO!?
WELL, I DID PUT A LOT OF HEART INTO THEM!!
ピー
PIII
OOPS.
WRONG BUTTON.

...AAAAAAAAUGH!
ALL DELETED
Deleted
I'M REALLY SORRY.
REALLY.
YOU'RE NOT SORRY!
THERE'S NO HEART IN THAT APOLOGY AT ALL!
SHIRA (INNOCENT)
しらっ
YOU DID THAT ON PURPOSE!
THAT WAS ALL MY BEST MATERIAL!
YOU EVIL—!
POKA (BONK)
ぽか
POKA
ぽか
POKA
ぽか
OKAY, EVERYONE, COME ON!
WE'RE GOING HOME!

KAI...
...IS SOMETHING WRONG?
YOU'RE SIGHING.
....
...NO...

...DID YOU STILL HAVE TROUBLE WITH THE HAUNTED HOUSE?
DID YOU MESS SOMETHING UP?
!?
NO!
NO WAY!
I MEAN, I DID, BUT—!!!
?
THAT'S NOT IT, OKAY!!
...IT'S NOT THAT.
IT'S JUST ...

......YOU CAN ORGANIZE YOUR THOUGHTS ...
...AND WHEN YOU'RE READY TO TALK, I'LL LISTEN.
EVEN IF THEY'RE NOT ORGANIZED...
...I'LL STILL LISTEN IF YOU WANT TO TALK.
... YEAH.
...... YEAH.
THANKS ...
UNTIL TODAY...

...I THOUGHT I KNEW MY WAY AROUND WOMEN.
WITH EVERY OTHER GIRL BEFORE, I KNEW EXACTLY WHAT I WANTED TO DO...
...AND I NEVER WORRIED ABOUT WHAT ANY OF IT MEANT.
NOW...
...FOR THE FIRST TIME IN MY LIFE, I'VE RUN INTO THE QUESTION ...

..."WHAT DOES IT MEAN TO FALL IN LOVE?"

Celebrating♥ *Hatsu * Haru*, Volume 2!

The Ichinose Corps (unofficial name)
are all such good kids it gives me warm fuzzies!
You can do it, Kai-kun! I'm rooting for you!

I got this adorable illustration from Yu_pon-sensei, the artist behind Chimi Chara!! Kai and his friends have become chimi characters!! Oooohhh! ♡♡

I've always been a big fan of Yu_pon-sensei's art, and I love it so much, I've collected a ton of chimi character merchandise. The capsule toys I talked about in the bonus pages of Volume 1 were almost all me collecting chimis, so do you have any idea how ecstatic I am to have my own characters made chimi!!? Yahooooo! ♫ They're all doing a "2" pose for Volume 2. The characters' individual personalities show in their poses—I'm impressed as always!!

Yu_pon-sensei, thank you so much!!!!

I will continue to dedicate the contents of my wallet to your chimi merch!!

CHAPTER 8

hatsu
haru

....
WHAT DOES IT MEAN TO FALL IN LOVE?
MY FEEL-INGS JUST KEEP GROW-ING...
......
......
...WITH NO HINTS AS TO WHAT TO DO ABOUT THEM.
Kai's Romantic Endeavors Support Group (3)
Tora
Kai is always sighing...
Mikki
I wonder if something happened with Takanashi at the theme park.
happened with Takanashi at the theme park.
Tora
Oh.
Tora
Oh no.
Mikki
!? What's wrong!?

Kai's Romantic Endeavors Support Group (3)
Tora
Kai's looking up "love" in the dictionary.
16:47
Tora
16:47
Mikki
Whooooooaaaaa—!!!!
16:48
LET'S TAKE A BREAK.
SUKKU (STAND)
WHAT? ALREADY?
BUT WE ONLY JUST STARTED.
I'LL GET SOME BARLEY TEA.
SURA (SLIDE)
KAI, LET'S HAVE SOME SNACKS.
THESE ARE REALLY GOOD!
I BROUGHT CHOCOLATE! YOU CAN HAVE IT, KAI!!
Chocolate
BAG: SOUR PLUM POTATO CHIPS
...THANKS...
WHAT THE—?
PIN (DING)
POOON (DONG)

HELLO!
!?
SUWA... SENSEI... AND... ...TAKA-NASHI !?
WHY...?
ONII— SENSEI GOT LOST, SO I SHOWED HIM HERE.
I'M MAKING A HOUSE CALL.
...WASN'T THAT SUPPOSED TO BE TOMOR-ROW?
WHAT !?
MY PARENTS AREN'T HOME RIGHT NOW.

AAAAHH, YOU'RE RIGHT!
MY HOUSE CALLS START TOMORROW!
ONII—SENSEI!!!
HOW CAN YOU BE SUCH AN AIRHEAD!?
....
I'M SO SORRY, ICHINOSE-KUN.
I'LL BE BACK TOMORROW!!
SORRY TO INTRUDE!
NOW, NOW, SENSEI!!
DON'T SAY THAT!
SINCE YOU'RE ALREADY HERE, PLEASE, COME IN!
I'LL MAKE US SOME TEA!
YOU TOO, RIKO-CHAN!
"RIKO-CHAN"?
YOU'RE SURE?
PLEASE, COME IN!

KARAN (CLINK)
カラン
WOW.
SO YOU WERE ALL STUDYING TOGETHER.
WHAT GOOD STUDENTS.
YEAH, WELL...
I WAS JUST COPYING TAKA AND TORA'S HOMEWORK.
THAT'S UNEXPECTED.
I THOUGHT YOU DEDICATED YOUR AFTER-SCHOOL HOURS TO DATES WITH DIFFERENT GIRLS EACH DAY.
HUH?
I USED TO.
WHOSE FAULT DO YOU THINK IT IS THAT MY AFTER-SCHOOL SELF IS NOW SO CLEAN AND PURE?

ICHINOSE-KUN MAY BE POPULAR, BUT HE'S ACTUALLY PRETTY DEVOTED.
EXCUSE ME?
WHAT ARE YOU TALKING ABOUT? THIS IS ICHINOSE.
THERE'S NO WAY.
...HEY.
NO, IT'S TRUE!
GIRLS KEEP TELLING HIM THEY LIKE HIM, BUT HE TURNS THEM ALL DOWN, BECAUSE HE'S IN LOVE WITH SOMEBODY ELSE!
ISN'T THAT RIGHT, ICHINOSE-KUN!!?

BAG: POTATO CHIPS, DELICIOUSNESS TOP-CLASS
OH!
...I-I'M SORRY. WAS THAT A SECRET?
...F—
FOR REAL!?
YOU'RE IN LOVE WITH SOME-ONE!?
THE VERY GIRL
....
...GH...
SUWAA-AAAAA!
Tora
How does Sensei know?
Mikki
Wow, Suwa's scary.
...

YOU KNOW, I NOTICED I HADN'T SEEN YOU WITH ANY GIRLS LATELY.
SO YOU FOUND SOME-ONE!
BUT FROM THE LOOK OF IT... YOU'RE NOT DATING HER YET?
THAT'S NOT LIKE YOU.
WHY NOT?
THE VERY GIRL
HE SAYS SHE'S IN LOVE WITH SOME OTHER GUY!
IT'S SUCH A SHAME, RIGHT? I MEAN, SHE'S EARNED THE LOVE OF ICHINOSE-KUN.
THE OTHER GUY
THE VERY GIRL
....
SUWA!
HEEEY!
DID YOU TELL HER YOU LIKE HER?
THE VERY GIRL
...NO...
NOT YET.
BUT YOU STRIKE ME AS THE TYPE WHO WOULD JUST GO FOR IT.
SO WHAT ARE YOU WAITING FOR?
....
—WHA ...

WHAT KIND OF NEW HELL IS THIS...?
RIGHT? IF SHE KNEW HE LIKED HER, SHE'D FALL FOR HIM IN A HEART-BEAT.
JUST BE YOUR USUAL COCKY SELF AND GO FOR IT.
Mikki
Takanashi!! Please stop! For his sake!
Tora
Thus, I have heard. At one time, the Buddha was dwelling in the Jeta Grove...
Mikki
Stop it!! Kai's not dead yet!!
...
...YOU...
...YOU WOULDN'T MIND...? IF I TOLD HER?

GO AHEAD.
IT'S NOT LIKE YOU NEED MY PERMISSION.
GO FOR IT!
?
WAAAAAHHH!
NO MORE! I CAN'T TAKE ANY MORE OF THIS!
THANKS FOR HAVING ME!
DOTA (STOMP)
TA
TA
OH!
EVERY-ONE'S HERE?
GOOD-BYE, MA'AM!
THANKS FOR HAVING US.
?
KAI.
YOU SHOULD AT LEAST SEE YOUR FRIENDS TO THE DOOR.
TOTA (TEP)
TOTA
WHAT'S THIS?
EXCUSE ME! I'M SUWA, ICHINOSE-KUN'S ASSISTANT TEACHER!
OH MY, SENSEI! I THOUGHT YOUR HOUSE CALL WAS TOMORROW ...?
OH!

YES, I MIXED UP THE DATES.
I'LL COME AGAIN TOMORROW.
OH, IS THAT ALL!
WELL, YOU'RE ALREADY HERE, SO WHY DON'T WE JUST HAVE IT NOW?
I'D FEEL BAD MAKING YOU COME BACK.
...UH...
PARDON MY INTRUSION.
OH, WHAT AN ADORABLE GIRLFRIEND!
YOU STU— SHE IS NOT!!!
I'M TAKANASHI, JUST A CLASSMATE!!
MIGHT YOU BE RIKO TAKANASHI-CHAN?
Y-YES, MA'AM.
YOU WENT TO GRADE SCHOOL WITH KAI.
I REMEMBER YOUR UNUSUAL NAME.
MY, HOW YOU'VE GROWN.
GROWN HOW?
SHE'S STILL A SHORTY.
STILL GRADE-SCHOOL SIZE.
KI (GLARE)

WELL, I'LL BE GOING NOW.
I WAS ONLY HERE TO SHOW SENSEI THE WAY.
DON'T SAY THAT. STAY FOR SOME CAKE.
I JUST GOT THIS FROM OUR NEXT-DOOR NEIGHBOR.
SHE BAKED IT HERSELF!
NOW, NOW, RIKO-CHAN!
WHAT ...?
URK!
BUT...
CAKE!!
REALLY? YOU'RE SURE YOU DON'T MIND!?
....
....
ONII-CHAN...

CAW!
CAW!
OH MAN, THAT WAS SO AWKWARD!
IT WAS PAINFUL.
BURORORO (VRROOOOM)
SORRY FOR ABANDONING YOU, KAI.
WILL HE BE OKAY?
GEEZ...
THIS IS WHY I TOLD YOU GUYS TO JUST LEAVE IT ALONE.
YEAH, BUT SHE'S SO OBLIVIOUS TO THE WHOLE THING.
YEAH... AND...
...SOMETHING STOOD OUT TO ME.

IS RIKO-CHAN IN LOVE WITH SOMEONE?
HE SAYS SHE'S IN LOVE WITH SOME OTHER GUY!
....
....
BASED ON THAT CON-VERSATION, I'D SAY YEAH.
....
....
AND HOW DID SUWA-SENSEI KNOW ALL THAT?
?
HEY, LET'S DROP THIS.
WE'VE ALREADY BEEN CAPPED OUT FOR THE DAY.
......
SIGH...
ピローン
PIRON (PRING)

IT'S A MESSAGE FROM OOSHIMA.
"WANT TO GO TO A MOVIE THIS SATURDAY?"
SHE SAYS.
"OF COURSE."
SEND.
GOOD FOR YOU, MIKKI.
LOOKS LIKE YOU MIGHT HAVE YOUR FIRST GIRLFRIEND.
OUR EFFORTS BORE FRUIT ON YOUR END, HUH?
YEAH...
I'M SORRY, KAI...
GARARARA (RATTLE)
WE'RE HOOOME!
OH, DEAR. LOOK AT THE TIME.

I'M SORRY! I DIDN'T MEAN TO STAY FOR SO LONG!
THAT'S ALL RIGHT. I'M THE ONE WHO KEPT YOU HERE.
LET'S GO HOME, RIKO-CHAN!
TOTA (TEP)
TOTA
I'M HOME!
GRANDMA! KAI-KUN!
!?
WEL-COME HOME.
WHAT? YOU ALL GOT HOME TOGETHER?

OH! GUESTS?
KAI'S TEACHER AND HIS CLASSMATE, RIKO-CHAN.
S-SORRY FOR IN-TRUDING.
WHAT'S THIS? LEAVING ALREADY?
SINCE YOU'RE HERE, STAY FOR DINNER!
IT'S ALREADY TIME!
DAD!!!
WHAT? MAY WE!?
ONII-CHAN!!!
HA HA HA.
SURE! STAY AND EAT! YOU TOO, LITTLE LADY!
......B-BUT...
DON'T BE SHY. HAVE SOME DINNER.
THERE'S A MILLION OF US ANYWAY. ONE OR TWO MORE WON'T MAKE MUCH DIFFERENCE.
GUESTS!
OR DOES YOUR FAMILY ALREADY HAVE DINNER READY FOR YOU?
....
NO.
THAT WON'T... BE A PROBLEM...

ALL RIGHT! THAT SETTLES IT!!
I'LL GO CHANGE.
WOW, THANK YOU SO MUCH.
OH, MOM.
I GOT THESE FROM A COWORKER THIS MORNING.
OH, WHAT LOVELY APPLES!
UGH, MY WHOLE FAMILY...
ANY LITTLE THING, AND THEY'RE ALL, "EAT THIS, EAT THAT!"
......
WHAT'S WRONG?
N-NOTHING!
....

OH MAN.

TOKU (POUR)
TOKU
I'M SO SURPRISED TO FIND OUT ICHINOSE-KUN HAS SUCH A BIG FAMILY!
IT'S KIND OF LIKE SAZAE-SAN!
HA-HA! MAYBE SO.
WE EVEN HAVE A MASUO.
SENSEI, IT'S TRUE. I'M THE MASUO OF THE FAMILY.
BUT MY REAL NAME IS KATSUO.
ACTUALLY.
WHAT!?
IT'S TRUE. AND ALL OUR NAMES ARE RELATED TO THE SEA.
KAI (OCEAN)
SANGO (CORAL)
NOT SO FAST.
USHIO (TIDE)
NAGISA (SEA-SHORE)
PASS THE SOY SAUCE, MASUO.
MY NAME IS KATSUO.
WHAT DO YOU THINK, SEN-SEI?
IS KAI GETTING ON WELL?
YES, SIR!!
HE'S EVEN WORKING AS CLASS REPRESEN-TATIVE. I APPRECIATE HIS HELP!
REALLY?
TRYING TO EARN EXTRA CREDIT?
NO!
SHE FORCED ME INTO IT.

HEY, TINY. YOU AFTER HIM?
!?
FORGET IT.
HE IS THE WORST WITH WOMEN.
I KNOW THAT!!
AND I'M NOT AFTER HIM!!!
HEY...
ALL RIGHT, THEN. GOOD.
TOKO (TODDLE)
とこ
TOKO
とこ
!
HOW OLD ARE YOU?
GRADE SCHOOL?
WHAT ......?
BWA-HA-HA!
SHE'S THE RIGHT SIZE FOR GRADE SCHOOL!!

I...I'M IN HIGH SCHOOL.
TAJI (FIDGET)
たじ
TAJI
たじ
WHAT!? LIKE KAI-KUN!?
BUT... SO LITTLE ...
?
HOO-HEH!
HEH HEH HEH!
HEY, COME ON.
WHY'RE YOU SO NERVOUS?
YOU SOUND SO STIFF.
SH...
SHUT UP.
RIKO-HYAN DOESHN'T GET TO SEE LI'L KIDS VERY MUCH, SHO SHE DOESN'T KNOW HOW TO TALK TO 'EM.
HIC!
WHAT? SERI-OUSLY?
SO EVEN YOU HAVE A WEAKNESS!
IT'S NOT A WEAK-NESS—

HERE YOU GO!
WAI—
STOP THAT!
BIKU (WINCE)
BIKU
BURA (DANGLE)
BURA
WHAT ARE YOU DOING WITH MY SON?
TOTA (TEP)
TOTA
TOTA
TOTA
I-I'M GOING TO THE REST-ROOM!!
FOR REAL? YOU'RE RUNNING AWAY?
SHE'S NOT REALLY HERSELF TODAY, IS SHE?
I'M SLEEPY.
HIC.
......
...I THINK SHE'S JUST NOT SURE HOW TO ACT.
MM?
WITH THE KIDS?
NO, MORE THAN THAT.

—THIS WHOLE HOUSE...
...HAS THIS LOUD, LIVELY FAMILY ATMOSPHERE.
COME ON, TIME FOR YOUR BATH.
NO! LATER!
AH?
MY, MY.
HUH...?
RIKO-CHAN IS AN ONLY CHILD.
IT'S JUST HER AND HER MOM, WITH HER MOM USUALLY AWAY AT WORK.
I KNOW IT'S NOT MY PLACE...
...BUT SOMETIMES I WISH THAT AKEMI-SAN AND I...
...COULD BE HER FAMILY.
BUT THAT JUST ISN'T ENOUGH.

—I THINK IT'S SOMETHING SHE ALWAYS WISHED SHE HAD.
ALTHOUGH SHE'D NEVER ACTUALLY ADMIT...
...THAT SHE'S LONELY.
THAT'S WHY...
...I WISH SHE COULD JUST GROW UP...
...FIND SOME-ONE SHE CARES ABOUT...
...AND GET A BIG FAMILY OF HER OWN. I REALLY WANT THAT FOR HER.
BUT I WOULD MISS HER.
ARE YOU STUPID?

TAKANASHI IS IN LOVE WITH YOU.
I BET SHE WANTS THAT EXACT FUTURE WITH YOU.
BUT MORE THAN THAT...
...SHE'S PROBABLY WISHING FOR THAT FUTURE FOR YOU AND AKEMI.
...YOU'RE WRONG.
EH?

SHE DOESN'T THINK YOU'RE NOT ENOUGH.
TAKANASHI DOES THINK OF YOU AS FAMILY. YOU REALLY MEAN A LOT TO HER.
...YOU... THINK SO?
HA-HA... THANKS, ICHINOSE-KUN.
YOU DON'T NEED TO THANK ME...
GAN (WHAM)
!?
HUH...? HEY!
JUST A...

KAAA (SNORE)
か
DID ONII-CHAN FALL ASLEEP!?
WHY I OUGHTTA ......!!
I THOUGHT YOU DIED.
OH!
YEAH...
UGH, HE KNOWS HE CAN'T HOLD HIS LIQUOR! BUT HE ALWAYS GETS CARRIED AWAY!!
I'M SORRY. IS IT OKAY IF I LET HIM SLEEP FOR A WHILE?
I THINK HE'LL WAKE UP SOON ENOUGH.
GUUU (ZZZZ)
ぐ
SORRY ABOUT THIS. WE'LL LEAVE AS SOON AS HE'S AWAKE.
...IT'S FINE.

SAWA (FWISH)
サワ…
....
THANKS...
...FOR DINNER.
NO...
ACTUALLY, I FEEL KINDA BAD.
MY PARENTS...
AH-HA-HA.
I WAS A LITTLE SURPRISED.

BUT THE FOOD WAS YUMMY, AND I HAD FUN.
...WELL, THAT'S GOOD, THEN.
SHE'S SO CUTE.
TCH.
—YOU KNOW, I NEVER...
... THOUGHT I'D SAY THIS ...
...BUT YOU SEEM LIKE YOU'D MAKE A GOOD DAD, ICHINOSE.
WHAA —?

I MEAN, IT'S JUST A FEELING I HAD, SEEING YOU TODAY.
LOOK.
DO YOU THINK A GUY IN HIS FIRST YEAR OF HIGH SCHOOL WOULD TAKE THAT AS A COMPLIMENT?
I DON'T!
—GOOD LUCK...
...WITH THAT GIRL.
WH—
DOKI (BADMP)
WHERE DID THAT COME FROM?
YOU USUALLY MOVE SO FAST, BUT NOW YOU'RE REALLY HOLDING BACK.
THAT MEANS YOU REALLY LIKE HER, RIGHT?

...I GUESS.
SO WHY NOT TELL HER HOW YOU FEEL, EVEN IF SHE DOES LIKE SOME-ONE ELSE?
ARE THEY DATING?
THE GIRL AND...
NO, THEY'RE NOT, BUT...
THEN YOU JUST HAVE TO GO FOR IT!
IT'S NOT EVERY DAY YOU FALL IN LOVE LIKE THAT!
THIS LITTLE ...
LIKE SHE'S NOT DOING THE SAME THING.
—

....
I DON'T KNOW...
HUH?
...WHAT I SHOULD DO—
SHE REALLY WANTS THIS GUY TO BE HAPPY...
...AND SHE'S CHOOSING HIS HAPPINESS OVER HER OWN FEELINGS.
AND...
...WHEN I SEE HER, PUTTING THIS GUY BEFORE HERSELF...
...I WONDER IF THAT'S WHAT IT MEANS TO LOVE SOMEONE.
AND I FREEZE UP...

WELL...
...I'M NOT HER, SO I COULDN'T SAY HOW SHE WOULD FEEL.
NO, YOU ARE HER...
DAMN... WHAT THE HECK?
BUT IF YOU CARE ABOUT HER THAT MUCH...
...THEN I'M PRETTY SURE SHE'D BE HAPPY WITH YOU.

YOU...
SERIOUSLY, IF YOU TELL ME THAT......
I... I'LL...!!!
TAKA-NASHI!
!?
GU (ZOOM)
SEE, THE TRUTH IS—
KAI-KUUUN!!!
DOSHI (GLOMP)
GUH-HURGH!
PEEL MY APPLE!

WHY ME?
DAMN IT!
WHERE'S YOUR MOTHER?
MOMMY'S TAKING A BATH.
AND GRANDMA'S WASHING THE DISHES!
HERE YOU GO. BE CAREFUL!
SHOULDN'T YOU TWO BE IN THE BATH TOO?
WE'RE GONNA TAKE ONE WITH YOU LATER!
きっぱり
KIPPARI (BLUNT)
WITH ME!!?
AWW, COME ON, MAKE *THAT! THAT!!*
FINE, IF I HAVE TO.
UGH.
たすっ
TASU (CHOP)
YAAAY!
むくり
MUKURI (RISE)
...OH, HEY. APPLES.
ONII-CHAN!

YOU CAN USE A KITCHEN KNIFE, ICHINOSE-KUN?
AH?
WHO DO YOU THINK I AM? I KNOW A FEW THINGS.
I'M IM-PRESSED.
I CAN'T USE A KNIFE WORTH BEANS.

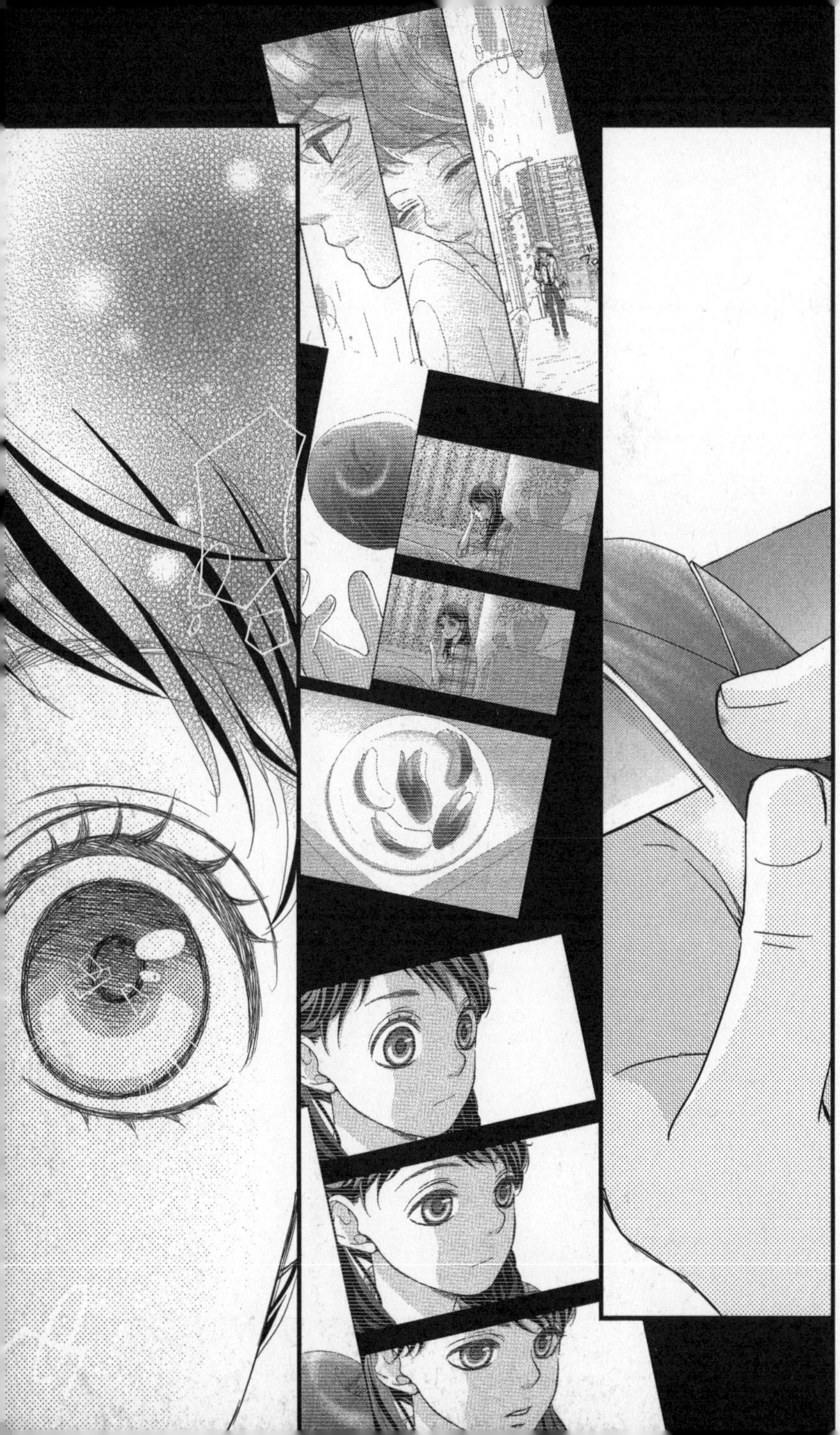

THERE, ALL DONE!!
YAY! BUNNIES!!
WOOOW! THAT'S PRETTY GOOD!!
YOU COULD MAKE A GOOD HOUSE-HUSBAND, ICHINOSE-KUN!
FIRST A GOOD DAD, NOW A HOUSE-HUSBAND.
THOSE AREN'T COMPLIMENTS, PEOPLE!
HUH?

THESE'RE SO MUCH PRETTIER NOW, KAI-KUN!
THEY WERE ALL MESSED UP BEFORE.
HOUSE-HUSBAND!
....
DO YOU KNOW WHAT YOU'RE SAYING?
HERE.
YOU SHOULD HAVE ONE TOO, TAKANASHI.
HMM?
WHAT'S WRONG?

....
NOTHING.
THANK YOU.
?
HATSU*HARU ② END

A FINE DAY FOR BUNGLING

Nevertheless, no amount of happiness...
...will get any work done if I'm asleep.
August 19th
uh...
And of course, before a deadline, I end up like this.
Eeeeeeeek!
So bad I can't even draw it.
I am currently blessed with the opportunity to draw two series at once, so there are some months where I have to draw more than one hundred pages...
...but thanks to everyone around me, I'm managing to push through.
Assistants, everyone concerned, thank you so much.
Grovel
I do get stressed out when I have to draw more than a hundred pages, but because I'm managing to get them all drawn somehow...
When I only have forty-five pages in a month, I don't know what insanity leads me to this thought, but...
I only have forty-five pages this month!!!
That's practically a vacation!!!
YAHOO!
And that's the trap I fall into.

In other words...

A person who doesn't sleep all day but who lives according to a regular routine and gets the job done!

That's what I want to be!!

Yes.

How can I do it...?

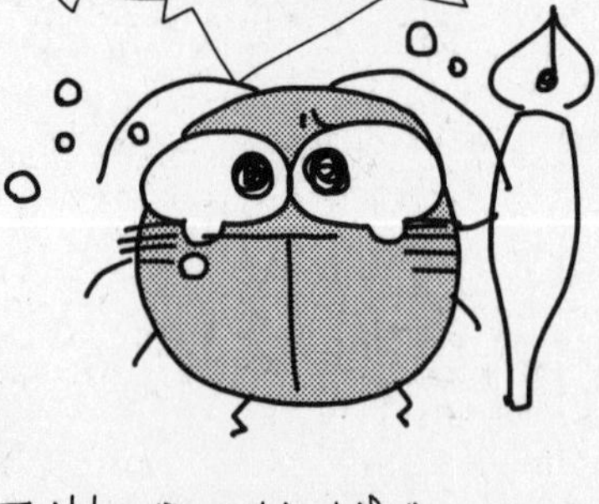

I may be a disappointing creator, but I hope you enjoy this Volume 2.

I look forward to your fan letters too.

Yen Press
1290 Avenue of the Americas
New York, NY 10104

Twitter ID→ shizukifujisawa
Blog → "Shizu Diary" shizukifujisawa.amebaownd.com

Special Thanks: Roku-san, Adacchan, Asamin, Kanchi, Mae-chan, Eda-chan, and my family

Translation Notes

PAGE 34

A ***danka*** is a family that lives within the jurisdiction of a Buddhist temple and supports it financially.

The name of the amusement park they go on their group date, **Waku-Waku Land**, is a play on the onomatopoeia for something that is thrilling or exciting.

PAGE 86

School events are usually a good time for **courage tests**. A spooky route will be chosen, and students will have to walk along it, alone or in pairs, in the dark.

The **Yotsuya Ghost Story**, or *Yotsuya Kaidan*, is a famous Japanese story about Oiwa, who was horribly disfigured and died, returning as a ghost to exact revenge on the people who wronged her. The story with the missing plate is about Okiku, the servant of a samurai who lusted after her. When she refused his advances, he tricked her into thinking she had lost one of his family's valuable plates—a mistake worthy of death. He offered to spare her life in exchange for marrying him, but she still refused and he killed her. She came back as a plate-counting ghost.

PAGE 110

Wall-pin: This is a famous anime and manga trope in which a male character will trap a girl of interest between him and a wall (*kabe*). This is a sudden move that usually comes with a *don* (wham) sound effect.

PAGE 142

Chimi Chara: A variant of "chibi," meaning "little," chimi characters are drawn in the cute, super-deformed style.

PAGE 147

In Japan, sometimes teachers will make **house calls** to visit their pupils. The main purpose for these visits are to get to know the student's family situation and to report the student's progress to his or her parents or guardians.

PAGE 153

Tora is reciting a Buddhist sutra, **"Thus I have heard,"** into his phone. Specifically, he is reading the Shorter Sukhāvatīvyūha Sūtra. He's a priest reading scriptures meant to help the dead peacefully pass on to the next life.

PAGE 164

A long-running comic and anime in Japan, ***Sazae-san*** is a comedy that deals with modern issues. Sazae-san and her husband, Masuo, live with her parents and little brother, Katsuo. A *sazae* is a kind of seashell.

hatsu ❀ haru 2

Shizuki Fujisawa

Translation/Adaptation: Alethea and Athena Nibley

Lettering: Lys Blakeslee

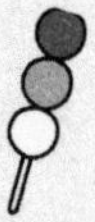

Yen Press
1290 Avenue of the America
New York, NY 10104

Visit us at yenpress.com ❀ facebook.com/yenpress ❀ twitter.com/yenpress
yenpress.tumblr.com ❀ instagram.com/yenpress

First Yen Press Edition: August 2018

Yen Press is an imprint of Yen Press, LLC.
The Yen Press name and logo are trademarks of Yen Press, LLC.

The publisher is not responsible for websites (or their content) that are not owned by the publisher.

Library of Congress Control Number:
2018935618

ISBN: 978-1-9753-5350-6

10 9 8 7 6 5 4 3 2 1

WOR

Printed in the United States of America